FUN FAX

Essential FACTS

Henderson
Woodbridge, England *Publishing*

COUNTRIES OF THE WORLD

EUROPE

Country	Population	Area Sq Km (Sq miles)	Capital	Language Spoken	Currency
Albania	3,000,000	28,750 (11,100)	Tiranë	Albanian	lek (100 qindarka)
Andorra	40,500	466 (180)	Andorre La Vielle	Catalan	franc & peseta
Austria	7,500,000	83,849 (32,377)	Vienna	German	schilling (100 groschen)
Belgium	9,500,000	30,509 (11,780)	Brussels	French & Flemish	franc (100 centimes)
Bulgaria	8,900,000	110,912 (42,826)	Sofia	Bulgarian	lev (100 stotinki)
Czechoslovakia	15,500,000	127,897 (49,383)	Prague	Czech	koruna (100 haleru)
Denmark	5,120,000	43,072 (16,630)	Copenhagen	Danish	krone (100 ore)
Finland	4,900,000	325,180 (125,557)	Helsinki	Finnish & Swedish	markka (100 pennia)
France	55,500,000	547,763 (211,500)	Paris	French	franc (100 centimes)
Germany	77,600,000	356,808 (137,771)	Bonn	German	mark (100 pfennigs)
Greece	10,000,000	117,840 (45,500)	Athens	Greek	drachma (100 lepta)
Hungary	10,700,000	93,030 (35,922)	Budapest	Hungarian	forint (100 filler)
Iceland	220,000	102,560 (39,600)	Reykjavik	Icelandic	krona (100 aurar)
Ireland — Republic of	3,500,000	70,283 (27,138)	Dublin	Irish & English	pound (100 pence)
Italy	57,300,000	301,257 (116,320)	Rome	Italian	lira
Liechtenstein	27,000	157 (61)	Vaduz	German	swiss franc
Luxembourg	395,000	2,586 (999)	Luxembourg	German, French & Luxemburgish	franc (100 centimes)
Malta	350,000	316 (122)	Valletta	Maltese &	pound (100 cents/ 1000 mils)
Monaco	26,500	1.8 (.69)	Monaco	French	french franc
Netherlands	14,500,000	41,179 (15,900)	Amsterdam	Dutch	guilder (100 cents)
Norway	4,200,000	323,737 (125)	Oslo	Norwegian	krone (100 ore)
Poland	37,500,000	312,600 (120,694)	Warsaw	Polish	zloty (100 groszy)
Portugal	10,300,000	92,082 (35,556)	Lisbon	Portuguese	escudo (100 centavos)

Country	Population	Area Sq Km (Sq miles)	Capital	Language Spoken	Currency
Romania	22,700,000	237,493 (91,700)	Bucharest	Romanian	leu (100 bani)
San Marino	21,800	61 (23.5)	San Marino	Italian	lira
Spain	38,800,000	504,642 (194,850)	Madrid	Spanish	peseta (100 centimos)
Sweden	8,350,000	449,964 (173,745)	Stockholm	Swedish	krona (100 ore)
Switzerland	6,500,000	41,288 (15,943)	Bern	German, French & Italian	franc (100 centimes)
United Kingdom	56,100,000	244,616 (94,450)	London	English	pound sterling (100 pence)
USSR	282,500,000	22,406,778 (8,650,160)	Moscow	Russian	rouble (100 copecks)
Vatican City State	1,000	.44 (.17)	Vatican City	Latin & Italian	lira
former Yugoslavia	23,250,000	252,515 (97,500)	Belgrade	Slovene, Macedonian, Serbo-Croat	dinar (100 paras)

ASIA

Country	Population	Area Sq Km (Sq miles)	Capital	Language Spoken	Currency
Afghanistan	14,500,000	647,497 (250,018)	Kabul	Dari & Pashtu	afghani (100 puls)
Bahrain	410,000	647 (250)	Manama	Arabic	dinar (1000 fils)
Bangladesh	103,500,000	143,998 (55,600)	Dacca	Bengali	taka (100 paise)
Bhutan	1,400,000	47,000 (18,148)	Thimphu	Dzongkha	ngultrum
Brunei	210,000	5,765 (2,226)	Bandar Seri Begawan	Malay	dollar (100 sen)
Burma	37,500,000	676,740 (261,230)	Rangoon	Burmese	kyat
Cambodia (Kampuchea)	6,230,000	181,034 (69,900)	Phnom Penh	Khmer	riel (100 sen)
China	1,050,000,000	9,583,924 (3,700,500)	Beijing Peking	Chinese, Mandarin	yuan (10 chiao/ 100 fen)
Cyprus	690,000	9,251 (3,572)	Nicosia	Greek, Turkish	pound (1000 mils)
Hong Kong	5,500,000	1,046 (404)	Victoria	Chinese, English	Hong Kong dollar
India	750,000,000	3,238,669 (1,250,500)	Delhi	Hindi, English	rupee (100 paise)
Indonesia	170,500,000	1,970,123 (760,695)	Jakarta	Bahasa	rupiah (100 sen)
Iran	47,600,000	1,646,528 (635,750)	Tehran	Persian	rial (100 dinars)
Iraq	16,250,000	434,921 (167,930)	Baghdad	Arabic	dinar (1000 fils)
Israel	4,300,000	20,768 (8,019)	Jerusalem	Arabic, Hebrew	shekel (100 agorot)

Country	Population	Area Sq Km (Sq miles)	Capital	Language Spoken	Currency
Japan	121,500,000	375,276 (144,900)	Tokyo	Japanese	yen
Jordan	3,500,000	91,941 (35,500)	Amman	Arabic	dinar (1000 fils)
Korea, North	20,100,000	120,539 (46,543)	Pyongyang	Korean	won (100 jun)
Korea, South	42,700,000	98,484 (38.028)	Seoul	Korean	won (100 jun)
Kuwait	1,850,000	17,818 (6,880)	Kuwait	Arabic	dinar (1000 fils)
Laos	3,700,000	236,716 (91,400)	Vientiane	Lao	kip (100 ats)
Lebanon	3,000,000	10,411 (4,020)	Beirut	Arabic	pound (100 piastres)
Macao	300,000	16 (6.2)	Macao	Chinese, Portuguese	pataca (100 avos)
Malaysia	16,200,000	329,746 (127,320)	Kuala Lumpur	Malay	dollar (ringgit) (100 cents)
Maldive Islands	195,000	298 (115)	Malé	Divehi	rupee (100 laris)
Mongolia	1,970,000	1,565,000 (604,294)	Ulan Bator	Mongol	tugrik (100 mongo)
Nepal	16,750,000	143,609 (55,450)	Katmandu	Nepali	rupee (100 pice)
Oman	1,200,000	248,021 (95,765)	Muscat	Arabic	rial (1000 baiza)
Pakistan	101,000,000	801,509 (309,475)	Islamabad	Urdu	rupee (100 peisas)
Philippines	57,360,000	299,988 (115,830)	Manila	Filipino	peso (100 centavos)
Qatar	355,000	11,175 (4,317)	Doha	Arabic	riyal (100 dirhams)
Saudi Arabia	10,994,000	2,249,000 (868,338)	Riyadh	Arabic	riyal (20 qursh)
Singapore	2,590,000	608 (235)	Singapore	English, Chinese, Malay, Tamil	dollar (100 cents)
Sri Lanka	16,250,000	65,610 (25,334)	Colombo	Sinhalese Tamil	rupee (100 cents)
Syria	10,960,000	185,180 (71,501)	Damascus	Arabic	pound (100 piastres)
Taiwan	19,500,000	36,178 (13,969)	Taipei	Chinese	dollar (100 cents)
Thailand	52,500,000	514,000 (198,471)	Bangkok	Thai	baht (100 satangs)
Turkey	51,500,000	781,100 (301,595)	Ankara	Turkish	lira (100 kurns)
United Arab Emirates	1,600,000	83,600 (32,280)	Abu Dhabi	Arabic	dirham (100 fils)
Vietnam	61,595,000	329,551 (127,245)	Hanoi	Vietnamese	dong (100 xu)
Yemen, North	6,350,000	192,947 (74,500)	San'a	Arabic	riyal (40 bogaches)
Yemen, South	2,200,000	336,687 (130,000)	Aden	Arabic	dinar (1000 fils)

NORTH AMERICA

Country	Population	Area Sq Km (Sq miles)	Capital	Language Spoken	Currency
Antigua and Barbuda	90,000	442 (171)	St John's	English	dollar (100 cents)
Bahamas	210,000	13,935 (5,381)	Nassau	English	dollar (100 cents)
Barbados	290,000	431 (166)	Bridgetown	English	dollar (100 cents)
Belize	185,000	22,966 (8,867)	Belmopan	English, Spanish	dollar (100 cents)
Canada	25,500,000	9,712,241 (3,750,045)	Ottawa	English, French	dollar (100 cents)
Costa Rica	2,600,000	50,909 (19,657)	San José	Spanish	colon (100 centimos)
Cuba	10,200,000	114,499 (44,210)	Havana	Spanish	peso (100 centavos)
Dominica	99,000	751 (290)	Roseau	English	dollar (100 cents)
Dominican Republic	6,400,000	48,735 (18,818)	Santo Domingo	Spanish	peso (100 centavos)
El Salvador	5,350,000	21,237 (8,200)	San Salvador	Spanish	colon
Grenada	95,000	331 (128)	St George's	English	dollar (100 cents)
Guatemala	8,500,000	108,889 (42,045)	Guatemala City	Spanish	quetzal (100 centavos)
Haiti	5,500,000	27,750 (10,715)	Port-au-Prince	French	gourde (100 centimes)
Honduras	4,400,000	112,088 (43,281)	Tegucigalpa	Spanish	lempira (100 centavos)
Jamaica	2,300,000	11,136 (4,300)	Kingston	English	dollar (100 cents)
Mexico	78,500,000	1,963,657 (758,198)	Mexico City	Spanish	peso (100 centavos)
Nicaragua	3,500,000	130,000 (50,197)	Managua	Spanish	cordoba (100 centavos)
Panama	2,200,000	76,650 (29,211)	Panama	Spanish	balboa (100 cents)
St Christopher (St Kitts) & Nevis	45,000	261 (101)	Basseterre	English	dollar (100 cents)
St Lucia	135,000	616 (238)	Castries	English	dollar (100 cents)
St Vincent and the Grenadines	125,000	388 (150)	Kingstown	English	dollar (100 cents)
Trinidad and Tobago	1,200,000	1,980 (5,130)	Port of Spain	English	dollar (100 cents)
United States	238,800,000	9,324,934 (3,600,500)	Washington DC	English	dollar (100 cents)

SOUTH AMERICA

Country	Population	Area Sq Km (Sq miles)	Capital	Language Spoken	Currency
Argentina	31,000,000	2,772,487 (1,070,500)	Buenos Aires	Spanish	peso (100 centavos)
Bolivia	6,200,000	1,096,822 (423,500)	La Paz — seat of government Sucre — legal	Spanish	peso (100 centavos)

Country	Population	Area Sq Km (Sq miles)	Capital	Language Spoken	Currency
Brazil	140,300,000	8,511,965 (3,286,727)	Brasilia	Portuguese	cruzeiro (100 centavos)
Chile	12,000,000	753,023 (290,754)	Santiago	Spanish	new peso (100 old escudos)
Colombia	29,500,000	1,138,914 (439,769)	Bogotá	Spanish	peso (100 centavos)
Ecuador	9,500,000	281,164 (108,562)	Quito	Spanish	sucre (100 centavos)
French Guiana	74,000	90,517 (34,950)	Cayenne	French	franc
Guyana	810,000	214,000 (82,632)	Georgetown	English	dollar (100 cents)
Paraguay	3,600,000	406,752 (157,059)	Asunción	Spanish	guarani (100 centimos)
Peru	20,000,000	1,285,165 (496,222)	Lima	Spanish	ita (100 centavos)
Surinam	390,000	163,552 (63,150)	Paramaribo	Dutch, English	guilder (100 cents)
Uruguay	3,000,000	182,587 (70,500)	Montevideo	Spanish	peso (100 centesimos)
Venezuela	17,320,000	912,033 (352,150)	Caracas	Spanish	bolivar (100 centimos)

AFRICA

Country	Population	Area Sq Km (Sq miles)	Capital	Language Spoken	Currency
Algeria	22,400,000	2,381,740 (919,662)	Algiers	Arabic	dinar (100 centimes)
Angola	8,500,000	1,246,700 (481,389)	Luanda	Portuguese	kwanza (100 lweis)
Benin	4,150,000	112,573 (43,483)	Porto Novo	French	franc
Botswana	1,120,000	582,727 (225,000)	Gaborone	English, Setswana	pula (100 thebe)
Burkina Faso	7,500,000	274,200 (105,877)	Ouagadougou	French	franc
Burundi	4,500,000	27,841 (10,750)	Bujumbura	French, Kirundi	franc
Cameroon	9,800,000	467,476 (180,500)	Yaoundé	French, English	franc
Cape Verde Islands	325,000	4,033 (1,557)	Praia	Portuguese	escudo Caboverdiano
Central African Republic	2,780,000	622,728 (240,445)	Bangui	French	franc
Chad	5,240,000	1,284,000 (495,791)	N'djamena	French	franc
Comoros	475,500	2,033 (785)	Moroni	French	franc
Congo	2,000,000	342,000 (132,057)	Brazzaville	French	franc
Djibouti	375,000	23,205 (8,960)	Djibouti	French	franc
Egypt	48,900,000	1,002,032 (386,900)	Cairo	Arabic	pound (100 piastres)

Country	Population	Area Sq Km (Sq miles)	Capital	Language Spoken	Currency
Equatorial Guinea	325,000	28,051 (10,831)	Malabo	Spanish	ekuele
Ethiopia	40,000,000	1,221,900 (471,812)	Addis Ababa	Amharic	dollar (100 cents)
Gabon	1,100,000	267,655 (103,346)	Libreville	French	franc
Gambia	750,000	11,295 (4,361)	Banjul	English	dalasi (100 bututs)
Ghana	13,500,000	238,270 (92,000)	Accra	English	cedi (100 pesewas)
Guinea	6,200,000	245,848 (94,926)	Conakry	French	syli
Guinea-Bissau	910,000	36,125 (13,949)	Bissau	Portuguese	peso
Ivory Coast	10,300,000	322,463 (124,513)	Abidjan	French	franc
Kenya	20,100,000	582,623 (224,960)	Nairobi	Swahili, English	shilling (100 cents)
Lesotho	1,500,000	30,355 (11,721)	Maseru	Sesotho, English	loti
Liberia	2,350,000	111,337 (42,989)	Monrovia	English	dollar (100 cents)
Libya	4,000,000	1,759,540 (679,412)	Tripoli	Arabic	dinar (1000 dirhams)
Madagascar	10,500,000	587,021 (226,650)	Antananarivo	French, Malagasy	franc
Malawi	7,100,000	104,243 (40,250)	Lilongwe	English, Chichewa	kwacha (100 tambala)
Mali	8,500,000	1,240,000 (478,801)	Bamako	French	franc
Mauritania	2,000,000	1,030,780 (398,000)	Nouakchott	Arabic, French	ouguiya (5 khoums)
Mauritius	1,000,000	2,071 (800)	Port Louis	English	rupee (100 cents)
Morocco	23,300,000	454,527 (175,500)	Rabat	Arabic	dirham (100 centimes)
Mozambique	14,200,000	793,804 (306,500)	Maputo	Portuguese	metical
Namibia	1,150,000	824,290 (318,284)	Windhoek	English, Afrikaans	South African rand
Niger	6,600,000	1,217,900 (470,250)	Niamey	French	franc
Nigeria	96,000,000	923,769 (356,695)	Lagos	English	naira (100 kobo)
Rwanda	6,320,000	26,338 (10,169)	Kigali	French, Kinyarwanda	franc
São Tomé and Principe	110,000	997,115 (385)	São Tomé	Portuguese	dobra
Senegal	6,700,000	196,192 (75,756)	Dakar	French	franc
Seychelles	89,000	398 (154)	Victoria	French, English	rupee
Sierra Leone	3,600,000	72,128 (27,850)	Freetown	English	leone (100 cents)
Somalia	6,300,000	637,657 (246,219)	Mogadishu	Somali, Arabic	shilling (100 cents)

Country	Population	Area Sq Km (Sq miles)	Capital	Language Spoken	Currency
South Africa	27,250,000	1,166,814 (450,525)	Pretoria – seat of government. Cape Town – legal capital	English, Afrikaans	rand (100 cents)
Sudan	23,500,000	2,505,728 (967,500)	Khartoum	Arabic	pound (100 piastres/ 1000 milliemes)
Swaziland	635,000	17,364 (6,704)	Mbabane	English, Swazi	emalangeni (100 cents)
Tanzania	22,750,000	945,018 (364,886)	Dodoma	English, Swahili	shilling (100 cents)
Togo	3,140,000	56,783 (21,925)	Lomé	French	franc
Tunisia	7,230,000	158,631 (61,250)	Tunis	Arabic French	dinar (1000 millimes)
Uganda	15,500,000	236,419 (91,285)	Kampala	English	shilling (100 cents)
Zaire	31,500,000	2,345,037 (905,455)	Kinshasa	French	zaire (100 mukuta/ 1000 sengi)
Zambia	6,950,000	752,614 (290,607)	Lusaka	English	kwacha
Zimbabwe	8,640,000	390,297 (150,700)	Harare	English	dollar (100 cents)

OCEANIA

Country	Population	Area Sq Km (Sq miles)	Capital	Language Spoken	Currency
Australia	15,850,000	7,684,492 (2,967,000)	Canberra	English	dollar (100 cents)
Fiji	705,000	18,275 (7,056)	Suva	Fijian, English	dollar (100 cents)
Kiribati	63,000	841 (325)	Tarawa	English, Gilbertese	Australian dollar
Nauru	8,000	21 (8.1)	Nauru	English, Nauruan	dollar (100 cents)
New Zealand	3,350,000	268,676 (103,740)	Wellington	English	dollar (100 cents)
Papua New Guinea	3,450,000	451,512 (174,336)	Port Moresby	English	kina
Solomon Islands	290,000	27,297 (10,540)	Honiara	English	dollar
Tonga	97,000	738 (285)	Nuku'alofa	English	pa'anga (100 senite)
Tuvalu	8,150	25 (9.7)	Fongafale or Funafuti	Tuvalu	Australian dollar
Vanuatu	125,000	14,763 (5,700)	Port Vila	Bislama, English, French	vatu
Western Samoa	197,000	2,835 (1,095)	Apia	Samoan English	tala (100 sene)

THE STATES OF AUSTRALIA

STATE	AREA		POPULATION	CAPITAL
	sq km	sq miles		
Capital Territory	2,432	939	245,600	Canberra
New South Wales	801,428	309,450	5,042,700	Sydney
Northern Territory	1,356,176	523,624	138,900	Darwin
Queensland	1,727,522	667,036	2,179,900	Brisbane
South Australia	984,377	380,091	1,290,900	Adelaide
Tasmania	67,897	26,215	437,300	Hobart
Victoria	227,618	87,883	4,075,900	Melbourne
Western Australia	2,527,621	975,973	1,382,600	Perth

THE CANADIAN PROVINCES AND TERRITORIES

PROVINCE OR TERRITORY	AREA		POPULATION	CAPITAL
	sq km	sq miles		
Alberta	661,188	255,300	2,344,600	Edmonton
British Columbia	948,560	366,240	2,530,000	Victoria
Manitoba	650,000	250,966	1,032,000	Winnipeg
New Brunswick	73,437	28,354	718,400	Fredericton
Newfoundland And Labrador	404,518	156,194	579,700	St John's
Northwest Territory	3,379,693	1,304,978	43,500	Yellowknife
Nova Scotia	55,491	21,426	841,200	Halifax
Ontario	1,068,587	412,584	9,047,900	Toronto
Prince Edward Island	5,657	2,184	122,000	Charlottetown
Quebec	1,540,687	594,863	6,572,300	Quebec
Saskatchewan	651,903	251,701	947,100	Regina
Yukon Territory	536,326	207,088	22,800	Whitehorse

THE STATES OF THE USA

STATE	AREA sq km	AREA sq miles	POPULATION	CAPITAL	FLOWER	BIRD
Alabama	133,915	51,705	4,021,000	Montgomery	Camellia	Yellowhammer
Alaska	1,518,800	586,412	521,000	Juneau	Forget-Me-Not	Willow Ptarmigan
Arizona	295,259	114,000	3,187,000	Phoenix	Saguaro Cactus	Cactus Wren
Arkansas	137,539	53,104	2,359,000	Little Rock	Apple Blossom	Mockingbird
California	411,047	158,706	26,365,000	Sacramento	Golden Poppy	California Valley Quail
Colorado	269,594	104,091	3,231,000	Denver	Rocky Mountain Columbine	Lark Bunting
Connecticut	12,973	5,009	3,174,000	Hartford	Mountain Laurel	Robin
Delaware	5,328	2,057	622,000	Dover	Peach Blossom	Blue Hen Chicken
Florida	151,939	58,664	11,366,000	Tallahassee	Orange Blossom	Mockingbird
Georgia	152,488	58,876	5,976,000	Atlanta	Cherokee Rose	Brown Thrasher
Hawaii	16,705	6,450	1,054,000	Honolulu	Hibiscus	Nene (Hawaiian Goose)
Idaho	216,430	83,564	1,005,000	Boise	Syringa	Mountain Bluebird
Illinois	149,885	57,871	11,535,000	Springfield	Violet	Cardinal
Indiana	93,993	36,291	5,499,000	Indianapolis	Peony	Cardinal
Iowa	145,790	56,290	2,884,000	Des Moines	Wild Rose	Eastern Goldfinch
Kansas	213,096	82,277	2,450,000	Topeka	Sunflower	Western Meadowlark
Kentucky	104,660	40,409	3,726,000	Frankfort	Goldenrod	Cardinal
Louisiana	125,674	48,523	4,481,000	Baton Rouge	Magnolia	Brown Pelican
Maine	86,156	33,265	1,164,000	Augusta	White Pine Cone And Tassel	Chickadee
Maryland	27,091	10,460	4,392,000	Annapolis	Black-Eyed Susan	Baltimore Oriole
Massachusetts	21,385	8,257	5,822,000	Boston	Mayflower	Chickadee
Michigan	251,493	97,102	9,088,000	Lansing	Apple Blossom	Robin
Minnesota	224,329	86,614	4,193,000	St Paul	Showy Lady's-Slipper	Common Loon

State	Area (km²)	Area (sq mi)	Population	Capital	Flower	Bird
Mississippi	123,514	47,689	2,613,000	Jackson	Magnolia	Mockingbird
Missouri	180,486	69,686	5,029,000	Jefferson City	Hawthorn	Bluebird
Montana	380,847	147,046	826,000	Helena	Bitterroot	Western Meadowlark
Nebraska	200,017	77,227	1,606,000	Lincoln	Goldenrod	Western Meadowlark
Nevada	286,297	110,540	936,000	Carson City	Sagebrush	Mountain Bluebird
New Hampshire	24,097	9,304	998,000	Concord	Purple Lilac	Purple Finch
New Jersey	20,295	7,836	7,562,000	Trenton	Purple Violet	Eastern Goldfinch
New Mexico	314,924	121,593	1,450,000	Santa Fe	Yucca	Roadrunner
New York	136,583	52,735	17,783,000	Albany	Rose	Bluebird
North Carolina	136,197	52,586	6,255,000	Raleigh	Dogwood	Cardinal
North Dakota	183,117	70,702	685,000	Bismarck	Wild Prairie Rose	Western Meadowlark
Ohio	106,764	41,222	10,744,000	Columbus	Scarlet Carnation	Cardinal
Oklahoma	181,089	69,919	3,301,000	Oklahoma City	Mistletoe	Scissor-Tailed Flycatcher
Oregon	251,418	97,073	2,687,000	Salem	Oregon Grape	Western Meadowlark
Pennsylvania	119,251	46,043	11,853,000	Harrisburg	Mountain Laurel	Ruffed Grouse
Rhode Island	3,139	1,212	968,000	Providence	Violet	Rhode Island Red
South Carolina	80,582	31,113	3,347,000	Columbia	Yellow Jessamine	Carolina Wren
South Dakota	199,551	77,047	708,000	Pierre	Pasqueflower	Ring-Necked Pheasant
Tennessee	109,411	42,244	4,762,000	Nashville	Iris	Mockingbird
Texas	691,027	266,807	16,370,000	Austin	Bluebonnet	Mockingbird
Utah	219,887	84,899	1,645,000	Salt Lake City	Sego Lily	Sea Gull
Vermont	24,900	9,614	535,000	Montpelier	Red Clover	Hermit Thrush
Virginia	105,716	40,817	5,706,000	Richmond	Flowering Dogwood	Cardinal
Washington	176,479	68,139	4,409,000	Olympia	Rhododendron	Willow Goldfinch
West Virginia	62,628	24,181	1,936,000	Charlestown	Rhododendron	Cardinal
Wisconsin	171,496	66,215	4,775,000	Madison	Wood Violet	Robin
Wyoming	253,596	97,914	509,000	Cheyenne	Indian Paintbrush	Meadowlark

PEOPLE

MONARCHS OF THE WORLD

The countries which still have hereditary monarchs are:

Country	Ruler	Came To Throne
Belgium	King Baudouin I	1951
Bhutan	King Jigme Singye Wangchuk	1972
Denmark	Queen Margarethe II	1972
Great Britain	Queen Elizabeth II	1952
Japan	Emperor Akihito	1989
Jordan	King Hussein II	1952
Liechtenstein	Prince Hans Adam II	1989
Luxembourg	Grand Duke Jean	1964
Monaco	Prince Rainier III	1949
Morocco	King Hassan II	1961
Nepal	King Birendra Bir Bikram Shah Dev	1972
Netherlands	Queen Beatrix	1980
Norway	King Harald V	1991
Saudi Arabia	King Fahd ibn Abdul Aziz	1982
Spain	King Juan Carlos I	1975
Sweden	King Carl XVI Gustaf	1973
Thailand	King Bhumibol Adulyadej	1946

NOBEL PEACE PRIZE WINNERS

1901 Henri Dunant (Switzerland) & Frederic Passy (France)
1902 Elie Ducommun and Albert Gobat (Switzerland)
1903 Sir William Cremer (UK)
1904 Institute of International Law
1905 Baroness Bertha von Suttner (Austria)
1906 Theodore Roosevelt (USA)
1907 Ernesto Moneta (Italy) & Louis Renault (France)
1908 Klas Arnoldson (Sweden) & Fredrik Bajer (Denmark)
1909 Auguste Beernaert (Belgium) & Paul d'Estournelles (France)
1910 Permanent International Peace Bureau
1911 Tobias Asser (Holland) & Alfred Fried (Austria)
1912 Elihu Root (USA)
1913 Henri La Fontaine (Belgium)
1914-16 No award
1917 International Red Cross
1918 No award
1919 Woodrow Wilson (USA)
1920 Léon Bourgeois (France)
1921 Karl Branting (Sweden) & Christian Lange (Norway)

1922 Fridtjof Nansen (Norway)
1923-24 *No award*
1925 Sir Austen Chamberlain (UK) & Charles Dawes (USA)
1926 Aristide Briand (France) & Gustav Stresemann (Germany)
1927 Ferdinand Buisson (France) & Ludwig Quidde (Germany)
1928 *No award*
1929 Frank Kellog (USA)
1930 Nathan Söderblom (Sweden)
1931 Jane Addams & Nicholas Butler (USA)
1932 *No award*
1933 Sir Norman Angell (UK)
1934 Arthur Henderson (UK)
1935 Carl von Ossietzky (Germany)
1936 Carlos de Saavedra Lamas (Argentina)
1937 Viscount Cecil of Chelwood (UK)
1938 Nansen International Office for Refugees
1939-43 *No award*
1944 International Red Cross
1945 Cordell Hull (USA)
1946 Emily Balch & John Mott (USA)
1947 Friends Service Council (UK) & American Friends Service Committee
1948 *No award*
1949 Lord John Boyd Orr (UK)
1950 Ralph Bunche (USA)
1951 Léon Jouhaux (France)
1952 Albert Schweitzer (France)
1953 George C. Marshall (USA)
1954 Office of the UN High Commissioner for Refugees
1955-56 *No award*
1957 Lester Pearson (Canada)
1958 Dominique Georges Pire (Belgium)
1959 Philip Noel-Baker (UK)
1960 Albert Luthuli (South Africa)
1961 Dag Hammarskjöld (Sweden)

1962 Linus Pauling (USA)
1963 International Red Cross & League of Red Cross Societies
1964 Martin Luther King Jr (USA)
1965 UNICEF (UN Children's Fund)
1966-67 *No award*
1968 René Cassin (France)
1969 International Labour Organization
1970 Norman Boriaug (USA)
1971 Willy Brandt (West Germany)
1972 *No award*
1973 Henry Kissinger (USA); Le Duc Tho (North Vietnam) — declined
1974 Sean MacBride (Ireland) & Eisaku Sato (Japan)
1975 Andrei Sakharov (Russia)
1976 Betty Williams & Mairead Corrigan (UK)
1977 Amnesty International
1978 Mohammed Anwar El Sadat (Egypt) & Menachem Begin (Israel)
1979 Mother Teresa of Calcutta (India)
1980 Adolfo Perez Esquival (Argentina)
1981 Office of the UN High Commissioner for Refugees
1982 Alva Myrdal (Sweden) & Alfonso Garcia Robles (Mexico)
1983 Lech Walesa (Poland)
1984 Bishop Desmond Tutu (South Africa)
1985 Physicians for Prevention of Nuclear War (USA)
1986 Elie Wiesel (USA)
1987 Oscar Arias Sanchez (Costa Rica)
1988 The United Nations Peacekeeping Forces
1989 Dalai Lama (Tibet)
1990 Mikhail Gorbachev (USSR)
1991 Aung San Suu Kyi (Burma)

BRITISH PRIME MINISTERS

Sir Robert Walpole (W)	1721-1742	Benjamin Disraeli (C)	1874-1880
Earl of Wilmington (W)	1742-1743	William Gladstone (L)	1880-1885
Henry Pelham (W)	1743-1754	Marquess of Salisbury (C)	1885-1886
Duke of Newcastle (W)	1754-1756	William Gladstone (L)	1886
Duke of Devonshire (W)	1756-1757	Marquess of Salisbury (C)	1886-1892
Duke of Newcastle (W)	1757-1762	William Gladstone (L)	1892-1894
Earl of Bute (T)	1762-1763	Earl of Rosebery (L)	1894-1895
George Grenville (W)	1763-1765	Marquess of Salisbury (C)	1895-1902
Marquess of		Arthur Balfour (C)	1902-1905
Rockingham (W)	1765-1766	Sir Henry Campbell-	
Earl of Chatham (W)	1766-1767	Bannerman (L)	1905-1908
Duke of Grafton (W)	1767-1770	Herbert Asquith (L)	1908-1915
Lord North (T)	1770-1782	Herbert Asquith (Cln)	1915-1916
Marquess of		David Lloyd-George	
Rockingham (W)	1782	(Cln)	1916-1922
Earl of Shelbourne (W)	1782-1783	Andrew Bonar Law (C)	1922-1923
Duke of Portland (Cln)	1783	Stanley Baldwin (C)	1923-1924
William Pitt (T)	1783-1801	James Ramsay	
Henry Addington (T)	1801-1804	MacDonald (Lab)	1924
William Pitt (T)	1804-1806	Stanley Baldwin (C)	1924-1929
Lord Grenville (W)	1806-1807	James Ramsay	
Duke of Portland (T)	1807-1809	MacDonald (Lab)	1929-1931
Spencer Perceval (T)	1809-1812	James Ramsay	
Earl of Liverpool (T)	1812-1827	MacDonald (Lab)	1931-1935
George Canning (T)	1827	Stanley Baldwin (Cln)	1935-1937
Viscount Goderich (T)	1827-1828	Neville Chamberlain	
Duke of Wellington (T)	1828-1830	(Cln)	1937-1940
Earl Grey (W)	1830-1834	Winston Churchill (Cln)	1940-1945
Viscount Melbourne (W)	1834	Winston Churchill (C)	1945
Sir Robert Peel (T)	1834-1835	Clement Atlee (Lab)	1945-1951
Viscount Melbourne (W)	1835-1841	Sir Winston Churchill (C)	1951-1955
Sir Robert Peel (T)	1841-1846	Sir Anthony Eden (C)	1955-1957
Lord John Russell (W)	1846-1852	Harold Macmillan (C)	1957-1963
Earl of Derby (T)	1852	Sir Alec Douglas-Home	
Earl of Aberdeen (P)	1852-1855	(C)	1963-1964
Viscount Palmerston (L)	1855-1858	Harold Wilson (Lab)	1964-1970
Earl of Derby (C)	1858-1859	Edward Heath (C)	1970-1974
Viscount Palmerston (L)	1859-1865	Harold Wilson (Lab)	1974-1976
Earl Russell (L)	1865-1866	James Callaghan (Lab)	1976-1979
Earl of Derby (C)	1866-1868	Margaret Thatcher (C)	1979-1990
Benjamin Disraeli (C)	1868	John Major (C)	1990-
William Gladstone (L)	1868-1874		

W = Whig. T = Tory. Cln = Coalition.
P = Peelite. L = Liberal. C = Conservative. Lab = Labour.

AUSTRALIAN PRIME MINISTERS

Edmund Barton	1901-1903	James H. Scullin	1929-1931
Alfred Deakin	1903-1904	Joseph A. Lyons	1932-1939
John C. Watson	1904	Robert Gordon Menzies	1939-1941
George Houston Reid	1904-1905	Arthur William Fadden	1941
Alfred Deakin	1905-1908	John Curtin	1941-1945
Andrew Fisher	1908-1909	Joseph Benedict Chifley	1945-1949
Alfred Deakin	1909-1910	Robert Gordon Menzies	1949-1966
Andrew Fisher	1910-1913	Harold Edward Holt	1966-1967
Joseph Cook	1913-1914	John Grey Gorton	1968-1971
Andrew Fisher	1914-1915	William McMahon	1971-1972
William M. Hughes	1915-1923	Edward Gough Whitlam	1972-1975
Stanley M. Bruce	1923-1929	John Malcolm Fraser	1975-1983
		Robert James Hawke	1983-

NEW ZEALAND P.M.

Henry Sewell	1856
William Fox	1856
Edward Stafford	1856-1861
William Fox	1861-1862
Alfred Domett	1862-1863
Frederick Whittaker	1863-1864
Frederick A. Weld	1864-1865
Edward W. Stafford	1865-1869
William Fox	1869-1872
Edward W. Stafford	1872
George Waterhouse	1872-1873
William Fox	1873
Julius Vogel	1873-1875
Daniel Pollen	1875-1876
Julius Vogel	1876
Harry Albert Atkinson	1876-1877
George Grey	1877-1879
John Hall	1879-1882
Frederick Whitaker	1882-1883
Harry Albert Atkinson	1883-1884
Robert Stout	1884
Harry Albert Atkinson	1884
Robert Stout	1884-1887
Harry Albert Atkinson	1887-1891
John Ballance	1891-1893
Richard John Seddon	1893-1906
William Hall-Jones	1906
Joseph George Ward	1906-1912
Thomas Mackenzie	1912
William F. Massey	1912-1925
Francis H. D. Bell	1925
Joseph G. Coates	1925-1928
Joseph G. Ward	1928-1930
George W. Forbes	1930-1935
Michael J. Savage	1935-1940
Peter Fraser	1940-1949
Sidney J. Holland	1949-1957
Keith J. Holyoake	1957
Walter Nash	1957-1960
Keith J. Holyoake	1960-1972
Sir John Marshall	1972
Norman Kirk	1972-1974
Wallace Rowling	1974-1975
Robert Muldoon	1975-1984
David Lange	1984-1989
Geoffrey Palmer	1989-

CANADIAN P.M.

Sir John MacDonald	1867-1873
Alexander Mackenzie	1873-1878
Sir John MacDonald	1878-1891
Sir John Abbott	1891-1892
Sir John Thompson	1892-1894
Sir Mackenzie Bowell	1894-1896
Sir Charles Tupper	1896
Sir Wilfred Laurier	1896-1911
Sir Robert L. Borden	1911-1920
Arthur Meighen	1920-1921
W. L. Mackenzie King	1921-1930
R. B. Bennett	1930-1935
W. L. Mackenzie King	1935-1948
Louis St Laurent	1948-1957
John G. Diefenbaker	1957-1963
Lester B. Pearson	1963-1968
Pierre Elliott Trudeau	1968-1979
Joe Clark	1979-1980
Pierre Elliott Trudeau	1980-1984
John Turner	1984
Martin B. Mulroney	1984-

AMERICAN PRESIDENTS

George Washington (F)	1789-1797
John Adams (F)	1797-1801
Thomas Jefferson (DR)	1801-1809
James Madison (DR)	1809-1817
James Monroe (DR)	1817-1825
John Quincy Adams (DR)	1825-1829
Andrew Jackson (D)	1829-1837
Martin Van Buren (D)	1837-1841
William H. Harrison (W)	1841
John Tyler (W)	1841-1845
James K. Polk (D)	1845-1849
Zachary Taylor (W)	1849-1850
Millard Fillmore (W)	1850-1853
Franklin Pierce (D)	1853-1857
James Buchanan (D)	1857-1861
Abraham Lincoln (R)	1861-1865
Andrew Johnson (U)	1865-1869
Ulysses S. Grant (R)	1869-1877
Rutherford B. Hayes (R)	1877-1881
James A. Garfield (R)	1881
Chester A. Arthur (R)	1881-1885
Grover Cleveland (D)	1885-1889
Benjamin Harrison (R)	1889-1893
Grover Cleveland (D)	1893-1897
William McKinley (R)	1897-1901
Theodore Roosevelt (R)	1901-1909
William H. Taft (R)	1909-1913
Woodrow Wilson (D)	1913-1921
Warren G. Harding (R)	1921-1923
Calvin Coolidge (R)	1923-1929
Herbert C. Hoover (R)	1929-1933
Franklin D. Roosevelt (D)	1933-1945
Harry S. Truman (D)	1945-1953
Dwight D. Eisenhower (R)	1953-1961
John F. Kennedy (D)	1961-1963
Lyndon B. Johnson (D)	1963-1969
Richard M. Nixon (R)	1969-1974
Gerald R. Ford (R)	1974-1977
James E. Carter (D)	1977-1980
Ronald Reagan (R)	1980-1989
George Bush (R)	1989-

F = Federalist. R = Republican.
DR = Democratic Republican.
D = Democratic. W = Whig. U = Union.

PLANET EARTH'S STATISTICS

Age: Approximately 4600 million years

Weight: Approximately 6000 million million million tonnes

Diameter: From Pole to Pole through the Earth's centre 12,794 km (7950 miles); across the Equator through the Earth's centre 12,837 km (7977 miles)

Area: Land 152,024,880 sq km (58,697,262 sq miles) = 29% of total surface
Water 358,003,850 sq km (138,826,360 sq miles) = 71% of total surface

Circumference: 40,020 km (24,868 miles) around Poles; 40,091 km (24,912 miles) around Equator

Volume: 1,084,000 million cubic km (260,000 million cubic miles)

Average land height: 841 m (2760 ft) above sea level

Average ocean depth: 3810 m (12,500 ft) below sea level

Density: 5.52 times water

Average temperature: 22°C (72°F)

Length of year: 365¼ days

Rotation time: 23 hours 56 minutes

Distance from Sun: 149,600,000 km (92,960,000 miles)

Atmosphere: Nitrogen — 78.5%; Oxygen — 21%

Crust: Oxygen — 47%; Silicon — 28%; Aluminium — 8%; Iron — 5%

LARGEST DESERTS IN THE WORLD

Desert	Location	Approx. area	
		sq km	sq miles
Sahara	North Africa	9,000,000	3,474,920
Australian	Australia	3,830,000	1,478,771
Arabian	Southwest Asia	1,300,000	501,933
Gobi	Central Asia	1,295,000	500,002
Kalahari	Southern Africa	520,000	200,772

THE WORLD'S LONGEST RIVERS

River	Main Location	Length	
		km	Miles
Nile	Egypt	6,650	4,132
Amazon	Peru, Brazil	6,437	4,000
Mississippi-Missouri	USA	6,020	3,741
Yenisey	Siberia	5,540	3,442
Yangtze	Tibet, China	5,494	3,434
Ob-Irtysh	W. Siberia	5,410	3,362
Zaire	Equatorial Africa	4,700	2,914
Hwang-ho (Yellow River)	China	4,640	2,883
Lena	Siberia	4,400	2,734
Mackenzie	Canada	4,241	2,635
Niger	W. Africa	4,180	2,600
St Lawrence-Great Lakes	Canada	4,023	2,500

HIGHEST MOUNTAINS

Mountain	Country	Height	
		m	ft
Everest	Nepal/Tibet	8,848	29,028
K2 (Chogori or Godwin-Austen)	Kashmir/China	8,611	28,250
Kanchenjunga	Nepal/Sikkim	8,598	28,208
Lhotse	Nepal/Tibet	8,501	27,890
Makalu	Nepal/Tibet	8,470	27,790
Dhaulagiri I	Nepal	8,172	26,810
Manaslu	Nepal	8,156	26,760
Cho Oyu	Nepal	8,153	26,750
Nanga Parbat	Kashmir	8,126	26,660
Annapurna I	Nepal	8,078	26,504

LARGEST ISLANDS

Island	Approx. area	
	sq km	sq miles
Greenland-Arctic Ocean	2,175,500	840,000
New Guinea-West Pacific	790,000	305,000
Borneo-Indian Ocean	750,000	289,500
Madagascar-Indian Ocean	587,000	226,600
Baffin Island, Canada-Arctic Ocean	508,000	196,000
Sumatra, Indonesia-Indian Ocean	470,000	181,500
Honshu, Japan-Northwest Pacific	230,000	88,800
Great Britain-North Atlantic	225,000	86,900
Victoria Island, Canada-Arctic Ocean	210,000	81,000
Ellesmere Island, Canada-Arctic Ocean	197,000	76,000

THE DEEPEST OCEANS

Ocean/Sea	Greatest depth	
	m	ft
Pacific Ocean	10,900	35,800
Atlantic Ocean	9,200	30,200
Indian Ocean	7,300	24,000
Arctic Ocean	5,600	18,500

THE LARGEST OCEANS

Ocean/Sea	Approx. area	
	sq km	sq miles
Pacific Ocean	166,100,000	64,131,000
Atlantic Ocean	84,500,000	32,625,500
Indian Ocean	73,400,000	28,340,000
Arctic Ocean	12,250,000	4,730,000

MAJOR WATERFALLS

Waterfall	River	Country	Drop	
			m	ft
Angel	Carrao	Venezuela	979	3,212
Tugela	Tugela	South Africa	948	3,110
Utigård	Jostedal Glacier	Norway	800	2,625
Mongefossen	Monge	Norway	774	2,540
Yosemite	Yosemite Creek	USA	739	2,425
Østre Mardøla Foss	Mardals	Norway	657	2,154
Tyssestrengane	Tysso	Norway	646	2,120
Cuquenán	Arabopo	Venezuela	610	2,000
Sutherland	Arthur	New Zealand	580	1,904
Kjellfossen	Naero	Norway	561	1,841

THE WORLD'S LARGEST LAKES

Lake	Area		Location
	sq km	sq miles	
Caspian Sea (salt)	371,800	143,550	USSR and Iran
Superior	82,350	31,800	Canada and USA
Victoria	69,500	26,830	Kenya, Uganda and Tanzania
Aral Sea (salt)	65,500	25,300	USSR
Huron	59,600	23,010	Canada and USA
Michigan	58,000	22,400	USA
Tanganyika	32,900	12,700	Tanzania, Zaire and Zambia
Great Bear	31,800	12,275	Canada
Baykal	30,500	11,780	USSR
Malawi	29,600	11,430	Malawi, Mozambique and Tanzania
Great Slave	28,500	10,980	Canada
Erie	25,700	9,930	Canada and USA
Winnipeg	24,500	9,465	Canada
Ontario	19,500	7,520	Canada and USA

The 9 planets are made up of 2 separate groups — the *terrestrial* planets of Mercury, Venus, Earth, Mars and Pluto and the *giant* planets of Jupiter, Saturn, Uranus and Neptune.

Here is a chart showing some facts about the planets in order of their distance from the Sun:

Planet	Mean distance from Sun (km)	Time to orbit Sun	Time to turn on axis	Mean temperature		Atmosphere
				Day	Night	
Mercury	58,000,000	88 days	59 days	400°C (750°F)	−170°C (−274°F)	None
Venus	108,000,000	224 days	243 days	400°C (750°F)		carbon dioxide
Earth	149,600,000	365¼ days	23.56 hours	22°C (72°F)		nitrogen & oxygen
Mars	228,000,000	687 days	24.37 hours	−20°C (−4°F)	−80°C (−112°F)	carbon dioxide
Jupiter	778,000,000	11.9 years	9.50 hours	Cloud Surface −150°C (−238°F)		hydrogen & helium
Saturn	1,427,000,000	29.5 years	10.14 hours	Cloud Surface −180°C (−292°F)		hydrogen & helium
Uranus	2,870,000,000	84 years	14 hours	Cloud Surface −21°C (−6°F)		hydrogen, helium & methane
Neptune	4,497,000,000	165 years	14 hours	Cloud Surface −220°C (−364°F)		hydrogen, helium & methane
Pluto	5,900,000,000	247.7 years	153 hours	−230°C (−382°F)		None

EXPLORATION 1963 - 1992

1963 June 16; USSR launch Vostok 6, with the first woman in space - Valentina Tereshkova - on board

1964 The USA's Ranger 7 obtains the first close-up pictures of the moon.

1965 Colonel Alexi Leonov makes the first space-walk from Voskhod 2.

1966 Feb. 3: USSR's Luna 9 makes the first soft-landing on the Moon.

June 1: USA's Surveyor 1 follows the USSR's soft-landing on the Moon.

1967 April 23-24: USSR's Vladimir Komarov is killed in space research when his ship Soyuz 1 crash-lands on Earth.

1968 Dec. 21-27: Three US astronauts become the first men to orbit the Moon in Apollo 8.

1969 July 21: USA launch Apollo-Saturn II and land Neil Armstrong and Edwin Aldrin on the Moon. Michael Collins remained inside the Command Module orbiting the Moon.

1970 Sept. 21: USSR's Luna 16 returns a moon sample to Earth.

1971 USA's Mariner 9 orbits Mars.

June 6: USSR launch first space station - Salyut 1.

1972 Dec. 7: USA launch Apollo 17, with the first scientist in space aboard.

1973 May 15: USA launch the first orbital space station - Skylab 2.

1974 USSR's Salyut 3 and 4 link up to form an orbiting observatory.

1975 July: USA's Apollo 18 links up in space with USSR's Soyuz 19.

1976 USA's Viking 1 and 2 spacecraft land on Mars, having been launched in 1975.

1977 USA's Voyager 1 and 2 unmanned spacecraft launched.

1978 USA's Pioneer Venus 1 and 2 launched and landed on Venus.

1979 Dec. 24: Ariane launched (European Space Agency satellite launcher)

1980 Nov.: USA's Voyager 1 successfully carries out a fly-by of Saturn.

1981 April 12: USA launch Columbia - the first re-usable manned space shuttle.

1982 USSR's Venera 13 and 14 land on Venus and discover surface soil to be similar to that of Earth's volcanic rock.

1983 USA's Challenger is crewed by Sally Ride - the first American woman in space.

1984 Astronauts carry out the first ever space-walk untethered to a spacecraft as repairs are performed on the Solar Max satellite.

1985 Two Soviet astronauts swap crew places following repair work on Salyut 7.

1986 Jan. 28: USA's Challenger space shuttle explodes, two minutes after blast off, killing all seven crew members.

Space probe, Giotto, launched to study the return of Halley's Comet.

Voyager 2 sends back detailed pictures of the moons of Uranus.

1988 USA launch Discovery space shuttle.

Two USSR astronauts return after a record 365 days in space.

USSR space shuttle Buran launched on back of the Energia booster rocket to make two orbits of the Earth.

1989 March 21: USA test Trident 2; it explodes four seconds after launch.

Aug. 3: USA's Voyager 2 discovers three new moons around Neptune.

1990 April: Hubble Telescope opens its eye on the universe beyond Earth's atmosphere.

Oct.: Astronauts on space shuttle Discovery launch European Space Station's Ulysses probe.

Dec.: Chinese journalist joined two Soviet cosmonauts on flight to the Soviet Space Station, Mir.

1991 May: Helen Sharman joined first British astronauts taking part in 8-day Anglo-Soviet mission to Mir. With two Soviet cosmonauts, she travelled to Mir aboard the Juno Soyuz rocket, launched at Baikonur, USSR.

1992 Robert Bondar is Canada's first woman in the Space Shuttle.

FACTS & FIGURES

ABBREVIATIONS

AA	Automobile Association	DJ	Disk Jockey
AAA	Amateur Athletic Association	EEC	European Economic Community
AD	anno domini (in the year of our Lord)	ER	Elizabeth Regina (the Queen)
AFA	Amateur Football Association	Esq	Esquire
		ESP	Extra Sensory Perception
am	ante meridiem (before noon); anno mundi (in the year of the world)	ETA	Estimated Time of Arrival
		FA	Football Association
BA	Bachelor of Arts	FC	Football Club
		GB	Great Britain
BBC	British Broadcasting Corporation	GMT	Greenwich Mean Time
		GP	General Practitioner
BC	Before Christ	GPO	General Post Office
C of E	Church of England	HM	His (Her) Majesty
CID	Criminal Investigation Department	hp	hire purchase; horse power
		HQ	Headquarters
CND	Campaign for Nuclear Disarmament	HRH	His (Her) Royal Highness
c/o	care of	ie	id est (that is)
Co	Company	IATA	International Air Transport Association
CV	Curriculum Vitae	IOU	I owe you
COD	Cash on Delivery	IQ	Intelligence quotient
DIY	Do It Yourself	IBA	Independent Broadcasting Authority

IRA	Irish Republican Army	PLC	Public Limited Company
JP	Justice of Peace	PM	Prime Minister
KO	Knock out	pm	post meridiem (afternoon); post mortem (after death)
KBE	Knight Commander (of the Order) of the British Empire		
		POW	Prisoner of War
KG	Knight of the Garter	PS	postscriptum
		PTO	please turn over
Ltd	Limited	QC	Queen's Counsel
MC	Master of Ceremonies	RAC	Royal Automobile Club
MBE	Member (of the Order) of the British Empire		
		RADA	Royal Academy of Dramatic Art
MOT	Ministry of Transport	RAM	Royal Academy of Music
MP	Member of Parliament; Military Police	RSA	Royal Society of Arts
		RC	Roman Catholic
mpg	miles per gallon		
mph	miles per hour	RIP	requiescat in pace (rest in peace)
NATO	North Atlantic Treaty Organisation		
		RSPCA	Royal Society for the Prevention of Cruelty to Animals
NB	nota bene (note well)		
NSPCC	National Society for Prevention of Cruelty to Children		
		RSVP	repondez s'il vous plait (please reply)
		SOS	Save our Souls
OBE	Officer (of the Order) of the British Empire	SRN	State Registered Nurse
		TUC	Trade Union Congress
pa	per annum (per year)		
PAYE	pay-as-you-earn	UN	United Nations
PVC	Polyvinyl Chloride		

UNESCO	United Nations Educational, Scientific and Cultural Organisation	WRAF	Women's Royal Air Force
UNO	United Nations Organisation	WRAC	Women's Royal Army Corps
vhf	very high frequency	YMCA	Young Men's Christian Association
VDU	visual display unit	YWCA	Young Women's Christian Association
VIP	very important person		

SIGNS, SYMBOLS & ABBREVIATIONS

=	is equal to	cm	centimetre(s)
≠	is not equal to	mm	millimetre(s)
≐	is approx equal to	m	metre(s)
		km	kilometre(s)
≡	is identical to	mg	milligram(s)
≯	not greater than	gm	gram(s)
>	greater than	kg	kilogram(s)
<	less than	ml	millilitre(s)
≮	not less than	cl	centilitre(s)
Σ	the sum of	l	litre(s)
∠	angle	sq	square
∞	infinity	cu	cubic
∈	is a member of the set of	oz	ounce
		lb	pound
∉	is not a member of the set of	cwt	hundred-weight
		in/"	inches
		ft/'	feet
∴	therefore	yd/^{x}	yards
∵	because		

TRADITIONAL ANNIVERSARY NAMES

Year	Name	Year	Name
1	paper	14	ivory
2	cotton	15	crystal
3	leather	20	china
4	fruit, flowers	25	silver
5	wood	30	pearl
6	iron, sugar	35	coral
7	wool, copper	40	ruby
8	bronze	45	sapphire
9	pottery	50	golden
10	tin, aluminium	55	emerald
11	steel	60	diamond
12	silk, fine linen	75	diamond
13	lace		

SIGNS OF THE ZODIAC

Capricorn	–	December 22-January 20
Aquarius	–	January 21-February 18
Pisces	–	February 19-March 20
Aries	–	March 21-April 20
Taurus	–	April 21-May 21
Gemini	–	May 22-June 21
Cancer	–	June 22-July 22
Leo	–	July 23-August 23
Virgo	–	August 24-September 22
Libra	–	September 23-October 23
Scorpio	–	October 24-November 22
Sagittarius	–	November 23-December 21

BIRTHSTONES

Month	Stone	Flower
January	Garnet	Snow Drop
February	Amethyst	Primrose
March	Bloodstone	Violet
April	Diamond	Daisy
May	Emerald	Lily of the Valley
June	Pearl	Rose
July	Ruby	Larkspur
August	Onyx	Poppy
September	Sapphire	Aster
October	Opal	Marigold
November	Topaz	Chrysanthemum
December	Turquoise	Holly

BEAUFORT WIND FORCE SCALE

Beaufort Number	Wind	mph	kph
0	Calm	1	1.6
1	Light air	1-3	1.6-5
2	Light breeze	4-7	6-11
3	Gentle breeze	8-12	13-19
4	Moderate breeze	13-18	21-29
5	Fresh breeze	19-24	30-39
6	Strong breeze	25-31	40-50
7	Moderate gale	32-38	51-61
8	Fresh gale	39-46	63-74
9	Strong gale	47-54	75-87
10	Whole gale	55-63	88-101
11	Storm	64-72	103-115
12	Hurricane	73 and more	116 and more

THE GREEK ALPHABET

Capital	Lower Case	Name	English Equivalent
A	α	Alpha	a
B	β	Beta	b
Γ	γ	Gamma	g
Δ	δ	Delta	d
E	ε	Epsilon	ĕ
Z	ζ	Zeta	z
H	η	Eta	ē
Θ	θ	Theta	th
I	i	Iota	i
K	k	Kappa	k
Λ	λ	Lambda	l
M	μ	Mu	m
N	ν	Nu	n
Ξ	ξ	Xi	x
O	o	Omicron	ō
Π	π	Pi	p
P	p	Rho	r
Σ	σ	Sigma	s
T	τ	Tau	t
Y	υ	Upsilon	u or y
Φ	ϕ	Phi	ph
X	χ	Chi	ch
Ψ	ψ	Psi	ps
Ω	ω	Omega	o

NATO ALPHABET

A	Alpha	J	Juliet	S	Sierra
B	Bravo	K	Kilo	T	Tango
C	Charlie	L	Lima	U	Uniform
D	Delta	M	Mike	V	Victor
E	Echo	N	November	W	Whisky
F	Foxtrot	O	Oscar	X	X-ray
G	Golf	P	Papa	Y	Yankee
H	Hotel	Q	Quebec	Z	Zulu
I	India	R	Romeo		

ROMAN NUMERALS

I	1	XVI	16	CD	400
II	2	XVII	17	D	500
III	3	XVIII	18	DC	600
IV	4	XIX	19	DCC	700
V	5	XX	20	DCCC	800
VI	6	XXX	30	CM	900
VII	7	XL	40	M	1,000
VIII	8	L	50	MM	2,000
IX	9	LX	60	MMM	3,000
X	10	LXX	70	MV	4,000
XI	11	LXXX	80	$\overline{V}$	5,000
XII	12	XC	90	$\overline{X}$	10,000
XIII	13	C	100	$\overline{L}$	50,000
XIV	14	CC	200	$\overline{C}$	100,000
XV	15	CCC	300	$\overline{D}$	500,000
				$\overline{M}$	1,000,000

Examples
1922   MCMXXII   1990   MCMXC

TEMPERATURE

To convert Fahrenheit to Celsius (Centigrade) and vice versa:

Fahrenheit to Celsius = Temperature $- 32 \times 5 \div 9$
Celsius to Fahrenheit = Temperature $\times 9 \div 5 + 32$

Quick glance conversion table:

°Centigrade		°Fahrenheit
100	– Boiling Point –	212
90		194
80		176
70		158
60		140
50		122
40		104
30		86
20		68
10		50
0	– Freezing Point –	32
– 10		14
– 20		– 4
– 30		– 22
– 40		– 40
– 50		– 58

MORSE CODE

Named after its American inventor, Samuel F.B. Morse (1791-1872) the Morse Code is a system of communication comprising dots and dashes, the dot being a signal of short duration, the dash three times this length. It was first used for sending messages by telegraph in 1844.

A	. _	M	_ _	Y	_ . _ _
B	_ . . .	N	_ .	Z	_ _ . .
C	_ . _ .	O	_ _ _	1	. _ _ _ _
D	_ . .	P	. _ _ .	2	. . _ _ _
E	.	Q	_ _ . _	3	. . . _ _
F	. . _ .	R	. _ .	4	. . . . _
G	_ _ .	S	. . .	5	. . . . .
H	. . . .	T	_	6	_ . . . .
I	. .	U	. . _	7	_ _ . . .
J	. _ _ _	V	. . . _	8	_ _ _ . .
K	_ . _	W	. _ _	9	_ _ _ _ .
L	. _ . .	X	_ . . _	0	_ _ _ _ _

SEMAPHORE

This form of communication is often used by sailors. Flags are placed in each hand and moved to different positions. Each different position denotes a letter of the alphabet.

TALLEST . . .

The tallest office building in the world is the *Sears Tower* in Chicago, Illinois. It has 110 storeys and stands 443m (1454ft) high. It has a population of 16,700, 103 lifts, 18 escalators and 16,000 windows.

The tallest hotel in the world is the *Westin Stamford* in Raffles City, Singapore. It has 73 storeys and stands 226.1m (74.9ft) high.

The tallest structure in the world is the guyed *Warszawa Radio* mast in Poland. It stands 646.38m (2120.8ft) tall and weighs an astonishing 550 tonnes!

THE SEVEN WONDERS OF THE WORLD

The Seven Wonders of the World were first compiled by Antipater of Sidon in the 2nd century BC.

1. Pyramids of Egypt

The only surviving wonder, built in about 2500 BC are The Pyramids of Egypt. These were constructed as royal tombs. The largest — the Pyramid of Cheops — stood 147 metres (482 feet) high.

2. Hanging Gardens of Babylon

There are no traced remains of the Hanging Gardens of Babylon in Iraq. These were built in about 600 BC and appeared to hang in the air because they were planted on terraces laid over arches — hence the name.

3. Statue of Zeus at Olympia

The Statue of Zeus at Olympia in Greece marked the site of the first Olympic Games in the 5th century BC. The statue, made out of marble, gold and ivory and standing 12 metres (40 feet) high was lost in a fire at Istanbul.

4. Colossus of Rhodes

The Colossus of Rhodes (sculptured in bronze by Chares of Lindus between 292-280 BC) stood 35 metres (117 feet) tall and featured the sun god Helios (Apollo). This was unfortunately destroyed by an earthquake in 224 BC.

5. Temple of Artemis (Diana) at Ephesus

The Temple of Artemis (Diana) of the Ephesians, was built at Ephesus in Turkey in about 350 BC. It was constructed of marble, stood 122 metres (400 feet) long and had more than 100 18 metres (60 feet) high columns. It was destroyed by the Goths in AD 262.

6. Mausoleum at Helicarnassus

The Mausoleum was erected in about 325 BC by Queen Artemisia in memory of her husband King Mausolus of Caria. It stood 43 metres (140 feet) high and remains may be found in the British Museum today.

7. Pharos of Alexandria

The world's earliest lighthouse — Pharos of Alexandria — stood 122 metres (400 feet) high. It was constructed of marble in about 270 BC and was destroyed by an earthquake in AD 1375.

THE LIVING WORLD

The largest animal is the Blue Whale, measuring more than 30 m long and weighing 160 tonnes, however, this size has not been seen for many years as they are extremely rare.

The smallest animals are Protozoans. These are single-celled creatures that can only be seen with a powerful microscope. 5000 of these would measure only 1 cm.

The oldest animal is the Giant Tortoise, which is known to have lived to 177 years.

The fastest fliers are ducks and geese which can exceed a speed of 65 mph. However, the Spinetail Swift has been recorded as flying at 106 mph.

The slowest flying bird is the American Woodcock, recorded as flying at 5 mph.

The fastest running animal is the cheetah, which can reach speeds of 65 mph.

The slowest moving mammal in the world is the three-toed Sloth which travels at 100 metres per hour.

The largest fish is the Whale Shark, which can reach up to 14m long.

The smallest fish (also a vertebrate) is the Dwarf Goby. These only grow to ½ inch in length.

The heaviest breeds of dog are the St Bernard and Old English Mastiff. The heaviest dog recorded is an Old English Mastiff, weighing 22½ stone, called Alcama Zorba of La Susa.

The tallest breeds of dog are the Great Dane and the Irish Wolfhound. The tallest dog on record was a Great Dane called 'Shamgret Danzas', which stood 41½ inches tall and weighed 17 stone.

The smallest breeds of dog are the Yorkshire Terrier, Chihuahua and the Toy Poodle. The smallest recorded dog was a Yorkshire Terrier, which died in 1945 and stood only 2½ inches tall and weighed an amazing 4 oz.

The oldest known dog on record was the Australian Cattle Dog called 'Bluey', who died at the ripe old age of 29.

The largest breed of cat is the Ragdoll. The heaviest recorded domestic cat was a male tabby called 'Himmy' who weighed in at nearly 47 lbs.

The smallest breed of domestic cat is the Singapura. A Siamese cross named 'Ebony-Eb-Honey Cat' is the smallest known cat, weighing only 1lb 2 oz.

The oldest cat ever recorded was 'Puss', who was 36 years old on 28 November 1939, but sadly he died on 29 November 1939.

INTERNATIONAL DISTINGUISHING SIGNS

Foreign registered vehicles should display an International distinguishing sign to signify the country of registration of the vehicle.

Index Mark	Country	Index Mark	Country
A	Austria	BR	Brazil
ADN	Yemen People's Democratic Republic (formerly Aden)	BRN	Bahrain
		BRU	Brunei*
		BS	Bahamas*
AFG	Afghanistan	BUR	Burma
AL	Albania	C	Cuba
AND	Andorra	CDN	Canada
AUS	Australia*	CH	Switzerland
B	Belgium	CI	Ivory Coast
BD	Bangladesh* (formerly East Pakistan)	CL	Sri Lanka* (formerly Ceylon)
		CO	Colombia
BDS	Barbados*	CR	Costa Rica
BG	Bulgaria	CS	Czechoslovakia
BH	Belize (formerly British Honduras)	CY	Cyprus*

Index Mark	Country		Index Mark	Country
D	Germany		I	Italy
DK	Denmark		IL	Israel
DOM	Dominican Republic		IND	India*
DY	Benin (formerly Dahomey)		IR	Iran
			IRL	Ireland*
DZ	Algeria		IRQ	Iraq
			IS	Iceland
E	Spain (including African localities and provinces)			
			J	Japan*
			JA	Jamaica*
EAK	Kenya*			
EAT	Tanzania*		K	Kampuchea (formerly Cambodia)
or	(formerly Tanganyia			
EAZ	& Zanzibar)		KWT	Kuwait
EAU	Uganda*			
EC	Ecuador		L	Luxembourg
ES	El Salvador		LAO	Lao People's Democratic Republic (formerly Laos)
ET	Egypt, Arab Republic of			
ETH	Ethiopia		LAR	Libya
			LB	Liberia
F	France (including overseas department and territories)		LS	Lesotho* (formerly Basutoland)
FJI	Fiji*		M	Malta*
FL	Liechtenstein		MA	Morocco
FR	Faroe Islands		MAL	Malaysia*
			MC	Monaco
GB	United Kingdom of Great Britain & Northern Ireland*		MEX	Mexico
			MS	Mauritius*
			MW	Malawi* (formerly Nyasaland)
GBA	Alderney* Channel			
GBG	Guernsey* Islands		N	Norway
GBJ	Jersey*		NA	Netherlands Antilles (formerly Curacao)
GBM	Isle of Man*			
GBZ	Gibraltar		NIC	Nicaragua
GCA	Guatemala		NL	Netherlands
GH	Ghana		NZ	New Zealand*
GR	Greece			
GUY	Guyana* (formerly British Guiana)		P	Portugal
			PA	Panama
H	Hungary		PK	Pakistan*
HK	Hong Kong*		PE	Peru
HKJ	Jordan		PL	Poland

Index Mark	Country	Index Mark	Country
PNG	Papua New Guinea*	T	Thailand*
PY	Paraguay	TG	Togo
		TN	Tunisia
RA	Argentina	TR	Turkey
RB	Botswana* (formerly Bechuanaland)	TT	Trinidad and Tobago*
RC	Taiwan		
RCA	Central African Republic	USA	United States of America
RCB	Congo (formerly French Congo)	V	Vatican City (formerly Holy See)
RCH	Chile	VN	Viet-Nam, Socialist Republic of (formerly North Viet-Nam and South Viet-Nam)
RH	Haiti		
RI	Indonesia*		
RIM	Mauritania		
RL	Lebanon		
RM	Madagascar (formerly Malagasy Republic)	WAG	Gambia
		WAL	Sierra Leone
RMM	Mali	WAN	Nigeria
RN	Niger	WD	Dominica* (Leeward Islands)
RO	Romania		
ROK	Korea, Republic of (formerly South Korea)	WG	Grenada* Windward
		WL	St Lucia* Islands
		WS	Western Samoa
ROU	Uruguay	WV	St Vincent and the Grenadines* (Windward Islands)
RP	Philippines		
RSM	San Marino		
RU	Burundi	YU	Yugoslavia
RWA	Rwanda	YV	Venezuela
S	Sweden		
SD	Swaziland*	Z	Zambia* (formerly Northern Rhodesia)
SF	Finland		
SGP	Singapore*	ZA	South Africa*
SME	Suriname* (formerly Dutch Guiana)	ZRE	Zaire
		ZW	Zimbabwe* (formerly Southern Rhodesia)
SN	Senegal		
SWA or ZA	Namibia* (formerly South West Africa)		
SY	Seychelles*		
SYR	Syria		

NOTE *In countries marked with an asterisk the rule of the road is drive on the left; otherwise drive on the right.

THE NATURAL ELEMENTS AND THEIR ATOMIC NUMBERS

Atomic Number	Element	Symbol
1	Hydrogen	H
2	Helium	He
3	Lithium	Li
4	Beryllium	Be
5	Boron	B
6	Carbon	C
7	Nitrogen	N
8	Oxygen	O
9	Fluorine	F
10	Neon	Ne
11	Sodium	Na
12	Magnesium	Mg
13	Aluminium	Al
14	Silicon	Si
15	Phosphorus	P
16	Sulphur	S
17	Chlorine	Cl
18	Argon	A
19	Potassium	K
20	Calcium	Ca
21	Scandium	Sc
22	Titanium	Ti
23	Vanadium	V
24	Chromium	Cr
25	Manganese	Mn
26	Iron	Fe
27	Cobalt	Co
28	Nickel	Ni
29	Copper	Cu
30	Zinc	Zn
31	Gallium	Ga
32	Germanium	Ge
33	Arsenic	As
34	Selenium	Se
35	Bromine	Br
36	Krypton	Kr
37	Rubidium	Rb
38	Strontium	Sr
39	Yttrium	Y
40	Zirconium	Zr
41	Niobium	Nb
42	Molybdenum	Mo
43	Technetium	Tc
44	Ruthenium	Ru
45	Rhodium	Rh
46	Palladium	Pd
47	Silver	Ag
48	Cadmium	Cd
49	Indium	In
50	Tin	Sn
51	Antimony	Sb
52	Tellurium	Te
53	Iodine	I
54	Xenon	Xe
55	Caesium	Cs
56	Barium	Ba
57	Lanthanum	La
58	Cerium	Ce
59	Praseodymium	Pr
60	Neodymium	Nd
61	Prometheum	Pm
62	Samarium	Sm
63	Europium	Eu
64	Gadolinium	Gd
65	Terbium	Tb
66	Dysprosium	Dy
67	Holnium	Ho
68	Erbium	Er
69	Thulium	Tm
70	Ytterbium	Yb
71	Lutecium	Lu
72	Hafmium	Hf
73	Tantalum	Ta
74	Wolfram	W
75	Rhenium	Re
76	Osmium	Os

77	Iridium	Ir	91	Protactinium	Pa
78	Platinum	Pt	92	Uranium	U
79	Gold	Au	93	Neptunium	Np
80	Mercury	Hg	94	Plutonium	Pu
81	Thallium	Tl	95	Americum	Am
82	Lead	Pb	96	Curium	Cm
83	Bismuth	Bi	97	Berkelium	Bk
84	Polonium	Po	98	Californium	Cf
85	Astatine	At	99	Einsteinium	Es
86	Radon	Rn	100	Fermium	Fm
87	Francium	Fr	101	Mendelevium	Md
88	Radium	Ra	102	Nobelium	No
89	Actinium	Ac	103	Lawrencium	Lr
90	Thorium	Th			

WEIGHTS AND MEASURES

AVOIRDUPOIS WEIGHT

16 drams (dr)	=	1 ounce (oz)
16 ounces	=	1 pound (lb)
14 pounds	=	1 stone (st)
28 pounds	=	1 quart (qr)
4 quarters	=	1 hundredweight (cwt)
20 hundredweight	=	1 ton

METRIC WEIGHT

1,000 milligrams (mg)	=	1 gram (g)
1,000 grams	=	1 kilogram (kg)
1,000 kilograms	=	1 tonne

LENGTH

12 inches (in)	=	1 foot (ft)
3 feet	=	1 yard (yd)
5.5 yards	=	1 rod, pole or perch
40 poles	=	1 furlong (fur)
8 furlongs	=	1 mile
1,760 yards	=	1 mile
3 miles	=	1 league

METRIC LENGTH

10 millimetres (mm)	=	1 centimetre (cm)
100 centimetres	=	1 metre (m)
1,000 metres	=	1 kilometre

METRIC MEASURES OF VOLUME

1,000 cubic centimetres	=	1 cubic decimetre
1,000 cubic decimetres	=	1 cubic metre

NAUTICAL MEASURE

6 feet	=	1 fathom
100 fathoms	=	1 cable
10 cables	=	1 nautical mile
6,080 feet	=	1 nautical mile
3 nautical miles	=	1 league

LIQUID MEASURE

4 gills	=	1 pint (pt)
2 pints	=	1 quart (qt)
4 quarts	=	1 gallon (gal)
8 gallons	=	1 bushel

METRIC LIQUID MEASURE

1,000 millilitres (ml)	=	1 litre (l)
1,000 cubic centimetres (cc)	=	1 litre

MEASURES OF AREA

144 square inches	=	1 square foot
9 square feet	=	1 square yard
30.25 square yards	=	1 square rod, pole or perch
40 square poles	=	1 rood
4 roods	=	1 acre
640 acres	=	1 square mile

METRIC MEASURES OF AREA

100 square metres	=	1 are
100 ares	=	1 hectare
100 hectares	=	1 square kilometre

MEASURES OF VOLUME

1,728 cubic inches	=	1 cubic foot
27 cubic feet	=	1 cubic yard

CONVERSION TABLES

WEIGHT

1 ounce	=	28.350 gram
1 pound	=	0.454 kilogram
1 ton	=	1.016 tonnes
1 kilogram	=	2.205 pounds
1,000 kilogram	=	0.984 ton

SURFACE MEASURE

1 square foot	=	0.093 square metre
1 square yard	=	0.836 square metre
1 acre	=	4,046.850 square metres
1 square mile	=	258.998 hectares
1 square metre	=	1.196 square yards
1 are	=	119.599 square yards
1 hectare	=	2.471 acres
1 square kilometre	=	0.386 square mile

LENGTH

1 inch	=	2.540 centimetres
1 foot	=	30.480 centimetres
1 yard	=	0.914 metre
1 mile	=	1.609 kilometres
1 centimetre	=	0.394 inch
1 metre	=	3.281 feet
1 metre	=	1.094 yards
1 kilometre	=	0.621 mile

MEASURE OF VOLUME

1 cubic inch	=	16.387 cubic centimetres
1 cubic yard	=	0.765 cubic metres
1 cubic centimetre	=	0.061 cubic inch
1 cubic metre	=	1.308 cubic yards

LIQUID MEASURE

1 Imperial pint	=	0.568 litre
1 litre	=	0.220 Imperial gallon
1 American pint	=	0.473 litre
1 litre	=	0.264 American gallon
1 Imperial gallon	=	4.546 litres
1 American gallon	=	3.785 litres

WORLD TIMES

0° longitude passes through Greenwich from where each additional 15° longitude represents one hour ahead to the east and one hour behind to the west. World time zones are approximate.

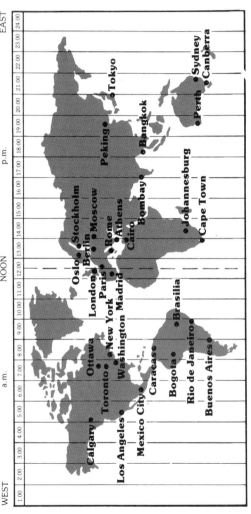

TIME

60 seconds	=	1 minute
60 minutes	=	1 hour
24 hours	=	1 day
7 days	=	1 week
4 weeks	=	1 month
12 months	=	1 year
365 days	=	1 year
366 days	=	1 Leap year
10 years	=	1 decade
100 years	=	1 century
1000 years	=	1 millennium

DAYS IN THE MONTH

Thirty days hath September,
April, June and November.
All the rest have thirty one
Except in February alone
Which has twenty eight days clear,
and twenty nine in each Leap Year.

Leap Years

Leap years occur every fourth year. To discover which is a leap year, divide the numbers of the year by four. In a leap year these numbers will divide evenly. e.g. 1988, 1992 etc.

Meridies is the Latin word for noon.
Ante means before : Post means after

From midnight to before noon is morning = ante meridiem = am

12 noon = midday

From noon to 12 midnight = afternoon = post meridiem = p.m.

THE HUMAN SKELETON

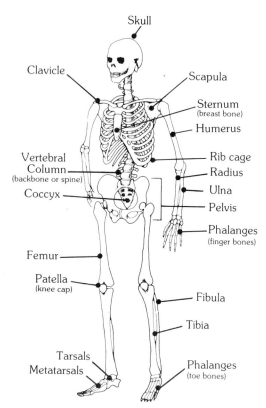

Skull

Clavicle

Scapula

Sternum
(breast bone)

Humerus

Vertebral
Column
(backbone or spine)

Rib cage

Radius

Coccyx

Ulna

Pelvis

Phalanges
(finger bones)

Femur

Patella
(knee cap)

Fibula

Tibia

Tarsals
Metatarsals

Phalanges
(toe bones)

The human skeleton consists of 200 bones. The bones are held together by joints called articulations, some of which allow movement of one bone on the other. At a moving joint the end of the bone is made of strong, smooth cartilage and lubricated by a fluid to allow it to move freely. Points where stress are applied are reinforced by fibrous tissue called ligaments. The spine has 26 bones which are linked to one another and make up the main frame of the body. They support the skull, ribs and two bone 'girdles' that support the arms, legs, shoulder blades and pelvis. The arms are connected to the shoulder blade and the legs to the pelvis.

The Olympics

The first Olympic Games were held in 776 BC at Olympia in Greece. They were held every four years until AD 393 at which time they were abolished by the Roman emperor of the time.

In 1894 Baron Pierre de Coubertin proposed that the Olympic Games be bought into play again on a modern footing. Therefore the first modern games took place in 1896 in Athens in a marble stadium built for the occasion.

The main events in the games consisted of track and field sports. The 1896 Olympics covered only nine sports with 43 events. This number had increased to 23 sports and 205 events by the 1972 Olympics.

Today the Olympics never contain less than 15 sports in any one Olympic Games.

1896	Athens, Greece	1952	Helsinki, Finland
1900	Paris, France	1956	Melbourne, Australia
1904	St Louis, USA	1960	Rome, Italy
1906	Athens, Greece	1964	Tokyo, Japan
1908	London, England	1968	Mexico City, Mexico
1912	Stockholm, Sweden	1972	Munich, West Germany
1920	Antwerp, Belgium	1976	Montreal, Canada
1924	Paris, France	1980	Moscow, USSR
1928	Amsterdam, Netherlands	1984	Los Angeles, USA
1932	Los Angeles, USA	1988	Seoul, South Korea*
1936	Berlin, Germany	1992	Barcelona, Spain
1948	London, England		*Some events in N. Korea

WINTER OLYMPICS

1924	Chamonix, France	1964	Innsbruck, Austria
1928	St Moritz, Switzerland	1968	Grenoble, France
1932	Lake Placid, United States	1972	Sapporo, Japan
1936	Garmisch, Germany	1976	Innsbruck, Austria
1948	St Moritz, Switzerland	1980	Lake Placid,
1952	Oslo, Norway		United States
1956	Cortina, Italy	1984	Sarajevo, Yugoslavia
1960	Squaw Valley,	1988	Calgary, Canada
	United States	1992	Albertville, France

THE COMMONWEALTH GAMES

The Commonwealth Games were first staged as the British Empire Games on 16th August 1930 in Hamilton, Canada and have been contested every four years (except 1942 and 1946) since. The eleven nations competing on that occasion were Australia, Bermuda, British Guiana, Canada, England, Ireland, Newfoundland, New Zealand, Scotland, South Africa and Wales.

YEAR	VENUE	SPORTS	COUNTRIES
1930	Hamilton, Canada	6	11
1934	London, England	6	16
1938	Sydney, Australia	7	15
1950	Auckland, New Zealand	9	12
1954	Vancouver, Canada	9	24
1958	Cardiff, Wales	9	35
1962	Perth, Australia	9	35
1966	Kingston, Jamaica	9	34
1970	Edinburgh, Scotland	9	42
1974	Christchurch, New Zealand	9	39
1978	Edmonton, Canada	10	46
1982	Brisbane, Australia	10	46
1986	Edinburgh, Scotland	10	26
1990	Auckland, New Zealand	10	55

MOTOR RACING
Formula One World Champions

Year	Champion	Year	Champion
1950	Giuseppe Farina (Italy)	1970	Jochen Rindt (Austria)
1951	Juan Manuel Fangio (Argentina)	1971	Jackie Stewart (Scotland)
1952	Alberto Ascari (Italy)	1972	Emerson Fittipaldi (Brazil)
1953	Alberto Ascari (Italy)	1973	Jackie Stewart (Scotland)
1954	Juan Fangio (Argentina)	1974	Emerson Fittipaldi (Brazil)
1955	Juan Fangio (Argentina)	1975	Niki Lauda (Austria)
1956	Juan Fangio (Argentina)	1976	James Hunt (England)
1957	Juan Fangio (Argentina)	1977	Niki Lauda (Austria)
1958	Mike Hawthorn (England)	1978	Mario Andretti (USA)
1959	Jack Brabham (Australia)	1979	Jody Scheckter (SA)
1960	Jack Brabham (Australia)	1980	Alan Jones (Australia)
1961	Phil Hill (USA)	1981	Nelson Piquet (Brazil)
1962	Graham Hill (England)	1982	Keke Rosberg (Finland)
1963	Jim Clark (Scotland)	1983	Nelson Piquet (Brazil)
1964	John Surtees (England)	1984	Niki Lauda (Austria)
1965	Jim Clark (Scotland)	1985	Alain Prost (France)
1966	Jack Brabham (Australia)	1986	Alain Prost (France)
1967	Denis Hulme (NZ)	1987	Nelson Piquet (Brazil)
1968	Graham Hill (England)	1988	Ayrton Senna (Brazil)
1969	Jackie Stewart (Scotland)	1989	Alain Prost (France)
		1990	Ayrton Senna (Brazil)

AMERICAN FOOTBALL

Super Bowl Results

Year	Venue	Winner		Loser	
1967	Los Angeles Coliseum	Green Bay Packers	35	Kansas City Chiefs	10
1968	Orange Bowl, Miami	Green Bay Packers	33	Oakland Raiders	14
1969	Orange Bowl, Miami	New York Jets	16	Baltimore Colts	7
1970	Tulane Stadium, New Orleans	Kansas City Chiefs	23	Minnesota Vikings	7
1971	Orange Bowl, Miami	Baltimore Colts	16	Dallas Cowboys	13
1972	Tulane Stadium, New Orleans	Dallas Cowboys	24	Miami Dolphins	3
1973	Los Angeles Coliseum	Miami Dolphins	14	Washington Redskins	7
1974	Rice Stadium, Houston	Miami Dolphins	24	Minnesota Vikings	7
1975	Tulane Stadium, New Orleans	Pittsburgh Steelers	16	Minnesota Vikings	6
1976	Orange Bowl, Miami	Pittsburgh Steelers	21	Dallas Cowboys	17
1977	Rose Bowl, Pasadena	Oakland Raiders	32	Minnesota Vikings	14
1978	Superdome, New Orleans	Dallas Cowboys	27	Denver Broncos	10
1979	Orange Bowl, Miami	Pittsburgh Steelers	35	Dallas Cowboys	31
1980	Rose Bowl, Pasadena	Pittsburgh Steelers	31	Los Angeles Raiders	19
1981	Superdome, New Orleans	Oakland Raiders	27	Philadelphia Eagles	10
1982	Silverdome, Pontiac, Michigan	San Francisco 49ers	26	Cincinnati Bengals	21
1983	Rose Bowl, Pasadena	Washington Redskins	27	Miami Dolphins	17
1984	Tampa Stadium	Los Angeles Raiders	38	Washingston Redskins	9
1985	Standford Stadium	San Francisco 49ers	38	Miami Dolphins	16
1986	Superdome, New Orleans	Chicago Bears	46	New England	10
1987	Rose Bowl, Pasadena	New York Giants	39	Denver Broncos	20
1988	San Diego Stadium	Washington Redskins	42	Denver Broncos	10
1989	Superdome, New Orleans	San Francisco 49ers	54	Denver Broncos	10
1990	Tampa Stadium	New York Giants	20	Buffalo Bills	19
1991	Minneapolis Metrodome	Washington Redskins	37	Buffalo Bills	24

SOCCER

World Cup Finals

Year	Venue	Winner		Runner-up	
1930	Montevideo, Uruguay	Uruguay	4	Argentina	2
1934	Rome, Italy	Italy	2	Czechoslovakia	1
1938	Paris, France	Italy	4	Hungary	2
1950	Rio de Janeiro, Brazil	Uruguay	2	Brazil	1
1954	Berne, Switzerland	W. Germany	3	Hungary	2
1958	Stockholm, Sweden	Brazil	5	Sweden	2
1962	Santiago, Chile	Brazil	3	Czechoslovakia	1
1966	Wembley, England	England	4	W. Germany	2
1970	Mexico City, Mexico	Brazil	4	Italy	1
1974	Munich, W. Germany	W. Germany	2	Netherlands	1
1978	Buenos Aires, Argentina	Argentina	3	Netherlands	1
1982	Madrid, Spain	Italy	3	W. Germany	1
1986	Mexico City, Mexico	Argentina	3	W. Germany	2
1990	Rome, Italy	W Germany	1	Argentina	0

TENNIS Wimbledon Champions

	MEN	WOMEN
1946	Yvon Petra (France)	Pauline Betz (US)
1947	Jack Kramer (US)	Margaret Osborne (US)
1948	Bob Falkenburg (US)	Louise Brough (US)
1949	Fred Schroeder (US)	Louise Brough (US)
1950	Budge Patty (US)	Louise Brough (US)
1951	Dick Savitt (US)	Doris Hart (US)
1952	Frank Sedgman (Aus)	Maureen Connolly (US)
1953	Victor Seixas (US)	Maureen Connolly (US)
1954	Jaroslav Drobny (Cz)	Maureen Connolly (US)
1955	Tony Trabert (US)	Louise Brough (US)
1956	Lew Hoad (Aus)	Shirley Fry (US)
1957	Lew Hoad (Aus)	Althea Gibson (US)
1958	Ashley Cooper (Aus)	Althea Gibson (US)
1959	Alex Olmedo (Peru)	Maria Bueno (Brazil)
1960	Neale Fraser (Aus)	Maria Bueno (Brazil)
1961	Rod Laver (Aus)	Angela Mortimer (GB)
1962	Rod Laver (Aus)	Karen Susman (US)
1963	Chuck McKinley (US)	Margaret Smith (Aus)
1964	Roy Emerson (Aus)	Maria Bueno (Brazil)
1965	Roy Emerson (Aus)	Margaret Smith (Aus)
1966	Manuel Santana (Spain)	Billie Jean King (US)
1967	John Newcombe (Aus)	Billie Jean King (US)
1968	Rod Laver (Aus)	Billie Jean King (US)
1969	Rod Laver (Aus)	Ann Jones (GB)
1970	John Newcombe (Aus)	Margaret Court (Aus)
1971	John Newcombe (Aus)	Evonne Goolagong (Aus)
1972	Stan Smith (US)	Billie Jean King (US)
1973	Jan Kodes (Cz)	Billie Jean King (US)
1974	Jimmy Connors (US)	Chris Evert (US)
1975	Arthur Ashe (US)	Billie Jean King (US)
1976	Bjorn Borg (Sweden)	Chris Evert (US)
1977	Bjorn Borg (Sweden)	Virginia Wade (GB)
1978	Bjorn Borg (Sweden)	Martina Navratilova (Cz)
1979	Bjorn Borg (Sweden)	Martina Navratilova (Cz)
1980	Bjorn Borg (Sweden)	Evonne Cawley (Aus)
1981	John MacEnroe (US)	Chris Evert-Lloyd (US)
1982	Jimmy Connors (US)	Martina Navratilova (US)
1983	John MacEnroe (US)	Martina Navratilova (US)
1984	John MacEnroe (US)	Martina Navratilova (US)
1985	Boris Becker (W Ger)	Martina Navratilova (US)
1986	Boris Becker (W Ger)	Martina Navratilova (US)
1987	Pat Cash (Aus)	Martina Navratilova (US)
1988	Stefan Edberg (Sweden)	Steffi Graf (W Ger)
1989	Boris Becker (W Ger)	Steffi Graf (W Ger)
1990	Stefan Edberg (Sweden)	Martina Navratilova (US)
1991	Michael Stich (Ger)	Steffi Graf (W Ger)